SEASONS
- An Allegory of the Stars -

Rennard Westley II

ISBN: 9781791942977

SEASONS

to anyone who has ever searched for love
and to everyone who has ever lost it

SUMMER

An Allegory of the Stars

with his footsteps on the fringe of heaven
drifting aimlessly through eternity
he summoned the Universe
and begged for a companion

to paint the cosmos with memories
to breathe life into new creations
to fill the void with colors
of worlds unknown

she thought the Sun might suffice
but he dared not suffer Icarus' fate

she suggested Mother Earth
but he preferred to not share
the weight of the world

then she presented the Rain
but he knew he would drown in her sorrows

at last the Universe proposed the Wind
as gentle as she was powerful
he had to see her for himself

SEASONS

how lucky are your lips

to taste heaven
coated in syntax

to sample
aphrodisiac
every time
someone asks
for your name

An Allegory of the Stars

i was drowning
in tears that
never leaked

a fallen saint
washed up
on the shore
of the promised land

- the day we met

SEASONS

many explore the sunkissed shore
and confuse their finds with gold
unaware that your true treasure
is buried in an ocean of thoughts

An Allegory of the Stars

i soak
daily
in thoughts
of You

SEASONS

excellence
is your aura

serenity spills
from your lips
divinity drips
from every pore

your speech
is laced
with legacy

your entire
existence
leaks lineage
of queens

An Allegory of the Stars

You are source itself
with enough light
and power
and energy
to keep the world
running

SEASONS

there is sunrise
in your pores

daylight
in your smile

You are summer
all by yourself

An Allegory of the Stars

may i take You out
to see the galaxy
the seduction
of her shine
the suns nesting
behind her smile
may i show You how
You appear to me

SEASONS

there is a tingling sensation
in my veins

i think mortals call them
butterflies

An Allegory of the Stars

i am intoxicated by your immortality

SEASONS

You smuggled
          an eternity
on your trip
          home
from heaven

An Allegory of the Stars

poems
have found me

and each one
says the same

they are here
for You

SEASONS

my lips
are the sahara

waiting

waiting

waiting

for your kiss

the rain
that comes
once
in a lifetime

An Allegory of the Stars

we plant seeds of wisdom
    harvest them with care
        soak them in emotions
           gift them to the Sun's lips

  knowing whatever blooms
      whatever thoughts take root
          our minds are fertile enough
                  for intimacy

SEASONS

all my waking moments
               are filled with thoughts
                             of You

An Allegory of the Stars

i put You on repeat
to commit You to my bones
with the rest of my favorite songs

SEASONS

You flatter me
how you fight sleep
trying to stay here
as heaven calls

as if You can't tell
the difference
between your home
and my arms

An Allegory of the Stars

some

      falls

             are fate's way

                    of moving us

                             forward

SEASONS

there
are
500
days
in
summer
and
i
spent
every
single
one
on
fire
for
You

An Allegory of the Stars

there are three words
rotting at the tip of my tongue

left unsaid
unattended
threatening
to expire
if not stored
somewhere safe

- is there space in your heart?

FALL

An Allegory of the Stars

the pair convened by starlight
sharing tales of boundless travel
the Moon begged the Sun to stay away
hoping to treasure the moment
when he refused, the Moon shifted tides
and buried their thoughts deep in the ocean

the eavesdropping Rain swelled with joy
as the clueless Sun returned to dry her tears
unable to explain with mere words
the Rain took the Sun by the hand
and colored the sky with scarlet
and coral and saffron and jade
and cerulean and indigo and violet

the Sun basked in amazement
the day never looked so majestic

SEASONS

I caught myself
as the earth
tilted on axis
and I wondered
whether to continue
falling for You

\- hesitation

An Allegory of the Stars

monday: You
tuesday: You
wednesday: You
thursday: You
friday: You
saturday: You
sunday: You

- daily gratitude list

SEASONS

I retired the Sun
and dismissed the alarm

You are enough
inspiration
to wake every day

An Allegory of the Stars

the Moon gave me a look
as if she could tell that
she no longer shifts
the tides of my heart
knowing I had found
another muse, in You

then the Moon wept
knowing the Stars
have whispered
about this day
for eons

SEASONS

the Moon kidnapped me
and all I talked about was
You
until the Sun rescued me

An Allegory of the Stars

I yearn for midnight
when the Moon
gossips
with the Stars
about your day
and the cosmos
ignite with jealousy

SEASONS

You are calligraphy
an art form
no longer studied
intricate beauty
no longer appreciated

An Allegory of the Stars

the galaxy gasped
Stars blushed
and the Sun
scoffed
at us-

acting like
a pair of mortals
in love

SEASONS

I love how your lips
spill glimpses of eternity
disguised as syllables

An Allegory of the Stars

You taught me
eyes and ears
are holy lands
every word is not
worthy of traveling

SEASONS

I traveled your thoughts
and discovered a land
of love
a language
of flowers
and I was no better
than christopher
staking claim of what long existed
before me

An Allegory of the Stars

what worlds
have You traveled
that your colors
are completely foreign

SEASONS

I can feel your influence
coursing through
the curve in my wrist
and the delicacy
in its dip
when my pen
caresses the canvas

- instrumental

An Allegory of the Stars

Maslow was incorrect
You are the foundation of my needs

SEASONS

there are miracles
in your mundane
divinity in your details
just look how your strands
stretch toward the Sun
and contort themselves in worship

An Allegory of the Stars

You are proof
God exists

SEASONS

from end
to end of
eternity
and every
inch between
You will find
my love for You

An Allegory of the Stars

You are
beauty
framed
in flesh

a portrait
of perfection
developed
in darkness

SEASONS

there is a sonnet in our silence

An Allegory of the Stars

your movement is a melody for my marrow
your rhythm is a remedy for the blues in my bones
your body is the ballad that keeps my heart beating

SEASONS

my heart is possessed by a stutter
stuck between a tick-
and a tock

lost in the
moment
we first
met

An Allegory of the Stars

I submit to your sentences
I surrender to the seduction of your lips
and the whip of your words

SEASONS

love is a phenomenon

An Allegory of the Stars

some nights I dream of flying
in others I dream of You
every morning my heart fails
to tell the difference

You complete me
and that is the beginning
of my problems

- Adam's paradox of the rib

An Allegory of the Stars

I look forward
to when You stop chasing

the light of day
the companionship of the Sun
and the warmth at the hem of his robes

to when you embrace
the darkness of your past
as the backdrop upon which
your color shines brightest

WINTER

An Allegory of the Stars

he loved everything about the Wind
from her calm caress to her careless
breezing through the world

everything was perfect
until it wasn't

the Wind grew restless
made to travel the length of the world
too anxious to be held (back)
by anything or anyone

he thought she might stay
if he could prove his love

so he offered his heart

filled with tears that never leaked
fragile as promise itself
burning with the fury of a thousand suns.

it was his only possession
but it wasn't enough

she left and he flew as long as he could
without her

SEASONS

she is enigma
with answers too complex
for comprehension

An Allegory of the Stars

I have searched
every fiber of my being-
every pore
every strand
every wrinkle
for solutions
to irreconcilable
problems

SEASONS

my heart
feels you
throbbing

thundering
in my veins

threatening
to leave
for good

An Allegory of the Stars

I remember
the vicious in your voice
the thunder in your throat
your once lush lips
laced with lightning
and assumptions

SEASONS

kidnapped tears rot
in a forgotten chamber
held hostage by a heart
whose only demand
is your touch

An Allegory of the Stars

somewhere there exists a world
where we still spill hopelessly
over one another

- reverie

SEASONS

we exploded from the blocks
with passion and purpose
but love is a marathon
and we learned that
you can't sprint
to forever

- pace

An Allegory of the Stars

we should have contained the embers
like a campfire lit with survival in mind
but we stoked the flames with our passion
and set the whole forest ablaze

- wildfire

SEASONS

you saved me from myself
just before we ruined us

An Allegory of the Stars

she birthed an apocalypse
through parted lips

an instant cataclysm
the minute divinity
disguised herself
as a jealous mortal

I swallowed an ocean

twenty thousand leagues
of memories we created

and I still thirst for you

An Allegory of the Stars

there is an ache
in my bones
traveling my spine
taking refuge
in my marrow
waiting patiently
to bloom

SEASONS

even on opposite end of eternity
with all of space between us
I still feel the gravity of your love

An Allegory of the Stars

I have everything I asked for
except you

meaning
I have all the things
I want
and none of what
I need

SEASONS

when I'm running
through your mind
where exactly do I go?

your imagination-
trampling what could have been?

do I trespass
the small of your back-
once reserved for my fingers?

does the earth shake beneath my soles?
do you ever stop me?

An Allegory of the Stars

I reached for an old book
and found a thought of you
in its place

- when borrowed books become stolen

SEASONS

we were nothing more
than propaganda
for hopeful romantics

An Allegory of the Stars

how long until you notice me
standing in your world
carrying all this love
that belongs to you

- my heart still has your name on it

when your love emptied out
my heart dried to stone
void of your nourishing waters
that once flowed unconditionally

but a part of me survived
and I don't know what's worse
the threat of you finding it
or how badly I want to give it to you

- survivor's remorse

An Allegory of the Stars

I gave my heart an indefinite leave
hoping it would return with no memory
of you

SEASONS

on the road to redemption
clutching a broken heart
surrounded by thieves

hands stretch from darkness
clawing grasping robbing pulling
every direction except forward

hunting for hearts
wayward as witchcraft
seduction of sirens

and still I give in
hoping to be reminded
of your touch

- follies (of the human heart)

An Allegory of the Stars

we built a house
out of excuses
and painted it
with promises

a monument
of nothingness

breathtaking,
but too hollow
to make a home

- sand castles

SEASONS

you returned my heart
but what of my senses?

An Allegory of the Stars

you were
unannounced thunder
splintering heaven
flooding the earth
with tears shed
for our failed romance

- windowpain

SEASONS

I stashed your scent
on the underside
of my pillow
so that the inevitable
dreams of you
would not reek of regret

- aroma therapy

An Allegory of the Stars

I caught a glimpse
of your crazy
in her eyes
and could not decide
whether to run or reminisce

- split decision

SEASONS

I fear the prospect of sleep
of running into you again
and being haunted by
how happy we once were

An Allegory of the Stars

we tiptoed across clouds

you showed me the world
but I needed to know

if I could fly on my own

SEASONS

you are the sweetest fruit in eden
I wonder what the world would be like
had I merely waited to taste you

An Allegory of the Stars

we were two disasters
wrapped in stratosphere
falling back to earth
more concerned with
the other's destruction
than our own safety

but what's worse
that we painted this tragedy together
or that we both agreed to call it love

SPRING

An Allegory of the Stars

it was a glorious descent
a downward spiral
ablaze with rage
fueled by confusion
burning with the fury
of a thousand suns

Mother Earth caught him
but she had no remedies for his problems
the Rain pitied him and cried tremendously

he looked to the edges of heaven
broken-hearted
and began picking up the pieces
bit by bit

a million what-ifs
and could-haves
but not a single regret

SEASONS

I no longer recognize
the world around me
I forgot what it looks like
to be the center of my own universe

An Allegory of the Stars

God must be fond of tragedies
why else would we get to pick
our own lovers

SEASONS

if I close my eyes
I can still find the trace
of your kiss in the breeze

An Allegory of the Stars

your voice is
a hospital bed of flowers
nursing me back to health
saving me from myself
and the insecurity
of silence

- trauma

SEASONS

my memory is stained with
the permanence of your ink

An Allegory of the Stars

sometimes I wonder
how to classify our story
was our romance a comedy or tragedy
was it even love to begin with

SEASONS

I am back to sleeping around
some nights with the Moon
others amongst the Stars
and with every new day
I hide from the Sun
lest he brag about
kissing You
good morning

An Allegory of the Stars

You trespass my mind every day

SEASONS

I no longer feel
You in my veins
and that is both
the good and
the bad news

An Allegory of the Stars

I once savored promise on your lips
not knowing lies could taste like honey

SEASONS

I consume thoughts of You whole
so that I won't taste the regret of time wasted

I used to burn for You
with a ferocious flame
it was feral and free
ablaze in glorious rage
a firestorm of feelings
fueled by the follies
of a drunken heart
and ignited by
the very thought
of You

SEASONS

there is a universe
where we still exist.

- the most romantic science fiction

An Allegory of the Stars

the way some things begin
is the way they will end
so our love burned
with the passion
of a thousand suns

SEASONS

the earth is round
so if we run forever
we will meet again
and it will prove to be
an explosion of time
and space and feelings
that no longer matter

- big bang theory

the only thing
I remember
before You
is a world
no longer
relevant

on one hand
she was heaven sent
and on the other
so was the plague

An Allegory of the Stars

the harvest needs the rain
just as much as the sunshine
and I needed your destruction
just as much as your daylight

SEASONS

what is the Universe
without the Sun
who am I without You

the answer to both
is a mystery full
of infinite possibilities

- dealing with the permanence of space

An Allegory of the Stars

thank God
for chaos
without it
I may have time
to think of You

SEASONS

only after You left
did I find the words
thank You
forgive me
I am sorry
I love You

- ho'oponopono

An Allegory of the Stars

perfection is not
the elimination
of flaws
but rather
acceptance
of them

SEASONS

I saw a picture of us
and could not recognize
the person beside You

- an alternate theory of growth

An Allegory of the Stars

do I owe my bloom to You
for transferring sunshine
with your touch and
conjuring rain
with your withdrawal

or to myself
for finding the light
that led to a world without You
and not drowning in a dream
that You had long left

SEASONS

You were my mirror
showing me not how much
your love for me lacked
but rather how much more
I needed to love myself

An Allegory of the Stars

even the most beautiful portraits
start as negatives in a dark room

SEASONS

like exhalation
after being submerged
too long in a deep story

like stillness
after the waves
of plot twists
end their assault

like conclusion
found in the last period
of an exhausting narrative

like finality
found at the end
of a book
with the permission
to begin another

- what closure feels like

An Allegory of the Stars

You are more than
a collection of poems

You are a masterpiece
coincidences curated
to show the universe
how to love herself
again and again
and again

You are a
forgotten psalm
an old testament
that showed me
not who God is
but rather where
I could find her
in myself

An Allegory of the Stars

even hearts
wrapped securely
in forever's fabric
can shatter into
a million pieces

even hearts broken
can be put back together
one poem at a time

58950977R00065

Made in the USA
Columbia, SC
29 May 2019